The
Legend
of
Light

The Felix Pollak Prize in Poetry
The University of Wisconsin Press Poetry Series
Ronald Wallace, General Editor

Now We're Getting Somewhere • David Clewell
    Henry Taylor, Judge, 1994
The Legend of Light • Bob Hicok
    Carolyn Kizer, Judge, 1995

The
Legend
of
Light

BOB HICOK

The University of Wisconsin Press

The University of Wisconsin Press
1930 Monroe Street
Madison, Wisconsin 53711

3 Henrietta Street
London WC2E 8LU, England

7   6   5   4   3

Printed in the United States of America
Library of Congress Cataloging-in-
    Publication Data
Hicok, Bob, 1960–
    The legend of light / Bob Hicok.
       90 pp.   cm. — (The Felix Pollak
       prize in poetry)
       ISBN 0-299-14910-2 (cloth: alk. paper).
       ISBN 0-299-14914-5 (pbk.: alk. paper)
       I. Title. II. Series.
    PS3558.I28L4   1995
    811'.54 — dc20   95-15836

for Eve

Contents

xi   Acknowledgments

3   Killing

5   In Her Hands

7   Inside

9   Neighbor

11   Weather

13   Extreme Measures

15   Rivera's Golden Gate Mural

18   Prodigal

19   Surgery

20   Duke

22   Memory

24   Waiting

26   The Dead

28   Rearview Mirror

30   Eight

34   85

35   Alice Wakes at Two and Looks Out the Window

36   530 Lakewood

38   Ten Years Dry

40   AIDS

42   My Job as It Relates to Bruegel's
             Netherlandish Proverbs

44   Voladores

46   Traffic Jam

48   Random Events

50   Visiting the Wall

54   Ohmy

56   Divorce

58   Learning of "It"

60   Nigger

62   Nurse

64   Man of the House

65   The Shrine

68   Ice Storm

71   Front Porch, Listening

73   Forecast

74   A Night at Modern Prototype

76   Dogfish Mother

78   Your Daughter

Acknowledgments

Boulevard	Rivera's Golden Gate Mural
Chelsea	Duke Ice Storm Voladores
Cream City Review	A Night at Modern Prototype Waiting Random Events
Indiana Review	Nurse
The Iowa Review	85 My Job as It Relates to Bruegel's *Netherlandish Proverbs* Nigger
The Kenyon Review	Your Daughter
The MacGuffin	Forecast
New Virginia Review	Rearview Mirror Ten Years Dry
Ploughshares	Killing
Poetry East	Man of the House The Shrine
Poetry Northwest	Front Porch, Listening In Her Hands Surgery
Prairie Schooner	Divorce Dogfish Mother
Quarterly West	Neighbor

River City	Ohmy
River Styx	Memory
	Prodigal
Southern Poetry Review	The Dead
Southern Review	Weather
Sycamore Review	530 Lakewood
Tar River Poetry	Visiting the Wall
Turnstile	Extreme Measures
Witness	AIDS
	Alice Wakes at Two and Looks Out
	the Window
	Eight

The
Legend
of
Light

Killing

As a boy I killed to kill, clubbed frogs
on the banks of a polluted river
as their knobby eyes protruded
through the foam of filth; turned sun
on ants, magnified Sol to fire, stalked them
with the glass as they scuttled to escape
my God-sized wrath. And if allowed a gun,
a .22 like Todd Clayton and Eric Granger had,
I'd have shot squirrels and jays, possum
and possibly Calvin Jamison as they did once,
in the leg and shoulder because he lisped,
played piano and spoke French, though primarily
because it occurred to them they could.
What changed my habits was a kick
in the ribs one lunch, more so the laughter
of those circling the fight, an impromptu ring,
and the words of the victor, who leaned low
and whispered that he owned my ass,
his face animated by a virulent form of bliss.
He was like linebackers I'd know later
who were calmed by violence, tackles
at peace only when the game was over
and there was blood on their jersey,
an ache where they'd been kneed or bit
and the memory in their flesh
of smashing against another body,
of screaming through a sweep as the play
collapsed around a common intention,
the need to compel others to do what they
didn't want to. I still know some of these guys
and the greatest compliment they can pay's

to say of an old opponent
that he killed them. This usually comes
after a few beers and the acknowledgement
that things aren't like they used to be,
knees and waists, hairlines and music,
which like philosophy is always said
to have been more authentic in the past.
I try to hurt nothing now, not centipede
or toad, the bats which get into the house
and circle in panic, unable to hear
their way out. Not because I'm good but because
the thought never leaves my body,
the child's lesson that not only
can I kill but will and want to.

In Her Hands

Palming his on-again
        off-again romance with life,
she breathes in synch with sys-
            and diastole, the sluggish oompa
of his failing heart. Here
        being's tangible, stripped
of narrative and afterthought,
            the smooth veil of skin pulled away

to reveal the body
        as contraption, labyrinth
we inhabit and by which
            we multiply, the frame giving soul
spine. Or is form all we are?
        She'll consider this later,
nights driving home or waking
            from the dream of a lily that cups

a ticking heart.
        Her own revs as she leans
into this stranger's chest
            to massage what had previously
been light, a blip pinging across a screen,
        an act placing her at the center
of his life though she doesn't
            know his name, the seasons he likes,

if his voice
                is sharp and vexing or soothes
like water slipping over skin.
                        She has pounded and zapped
these wounded valentines,
                sparked stiffs, those about
to be given a berth in the cool room,
                        brought them back for a chance

to hum and grouse,
                to search for the rabbit in the moon
again. But not like this: to hold
                a heart in her hands, beggar
trying to squeeze out the coin
                of hour or minute, stunned
by the thump that toggles, that vanishes
                        and returns, by the wandering signature

of his heart's jazz. Then
                to feel him die, to rest her hands
inside his body when there is only
                body, if this isn't all there ever was,
and watch as he's stapled shut,
                sealed up like a room from which
even light is barred. When the others leave
                she leans against a wall and notices

she wears his blood
                like a garish dress. Removing
the gown, she spreads it over his chest,
                        over the wound that couldn't save him,
and touches his lips
                with the back of two fingers
as she does her husband's when scared
                by how still he is sleeping.

Inside

I've a matryoshka doll on my mantle, Lenin
inside Stalin
      inside Brezhnev
         inside Gorbachev,
finally Yeltsin who looks like a bowling pin
with a tie. This homunculus of Soviet politics
is a greater attraction than my Cowardly Lion
and Scarecrow dolls, which can't be peeled
to a face staring back with the determination
of revolution. Most guests pull it down
and apart, separate heads from bodies
and spread the carnage across the table,
adults trying to guess who's who and usually
getting it wrong, suggesting Sakharov, Molotov,
even Nureyev once. Picture Lenin in tights,
Gorbachev at the bar, Stalin hoisting
Mother Russia above the stage, a ballerina
in work boots, a skeleton dressed for Gulag.
But the interest in the doll isn't particular.
It could be the Marx or Ringling Brothers,
the Swiss Family Robinson, Klimt in the belly
of Monet in the gut of Magritte. It reflects
our habit of looking for what's least,
the shell-game of quark and boson, W and Z,
identity sought in lobe and synapse,
the neurochemical soup. None of which
fulfills with the sense of an ending, each
smaller thing suggesting others, universes
hiding in the womb of atoms, eternities
buried in the eye of God. Yet beneath
Stalin's pipe, Gorbachev's birthmark,

Yeltsin's rummy face, is the irreducible image
of an axe painted on Lenin's side, the blade
dripping blood as if to say you need
cut no deeper for truth.

Neighbor

A man lives under the Beakes bridge. I drive over him
      every day. His hair's
like a troll's I had once, a thicket though not purple.
      Curled fetal, he sleeps
with his back to the river. I see him when I run, when
      I chase my breath
to stay alive. He has a radio I've never heard croon.
      Perhaps he's an aficionado
of silence. He doesn't wear foil on his head. Does not
      spread the flower of his hand
for coin. Not that I've seen and we are neighbors.
      I pass his house
on my way to breakfast, to buy shoes, tan or black
      lace-ups, to drive
into what's called the country but is really the city
      spread out like paint
on canvas. I live in an area where cities are growing
      together. The term used
is megalopolis. Everything will have to get bigger.
      Super-heroes. Air.
Stars if we're to see them ever again. Last night
      as I ran over the bridge
I saw that a tree had split, that the fallen half
      now dips into the river.
Around one branch ice had formed, a block the size
      of Sonja Henie's thigh.
I wondered if he watched the ice form, if the accretion
      was like TV to him.
He's lived here two years. One summer I saw him strip
      and wade into the river,
sit down and face the flow as if meeting his god
      head on. I wanted to stay

and stare but couldn't. Perhaps you've looked into a window
      just as a shirt
was removed or a shout cracked the egg of night's calm,
      and despite groin
or mind twitch, moved on. Though possibly as you did,
      you too couldn't help
a last look. He didn't sing or splash but threw his head back
      and drifted
under the water. As if baptized, as if pulled down
      by the flow which touches
like music, which cuts its home through rock and is gone.

Weather

My grandmother's on the phone
announcing the feel of snow in her bones.
Her county's
still a small world, cableless and dry,
its people antique, every quilting and haircut
a ruse
to talk health
and conduct the ritual seance of youth.
My bones confide nothing.
I'm aware they're there
only because my posture's
better than soup.
By the time dishes are done
the news will be a cold cup of coffee.
Even the dead will know.
Since calling the blizzard of '58
she's never missed,
a marvel to everyone
but the Rev. Hammond, whose eyes
were closed to the miraculous
by Vatican II.
As the first flakes
shake out of the sky,
I try to follow one to the ground,
to witness its secret life
before it melts
or melds into sameness,
the fear of my life.
My grandmother
blows on the window
and draws an eye in her condensed breath

as she dials another number.
The merely sane will take cover.
The wise will go upstairs,
undo buttons and hair,
fold themselves
within the covenant of flesh
and make love
wilder than any weather.

Extreme Measures

Blood was once thought a cure for epilepsy
and some Romans,
possessed by the disorder,
sucked the wounds of defeated gladiators.
Picture a Senator, vampire by prescription,
leaning over a dying man,
drinking the remedy for the storms
which throw his body down,
straighten his spine, shoot out his tongue
and often leave no memory of the event,
slicing away tiny portions of his life.
Blood's now asylum for a virus
scrawnier than a wavelength of visible light,
an indiscriminate parasite
which views the needled
and pimped
and loved
alike.
Desperate, some with AIDS
pop nerve-wasting drugs,
drink urine, shock flesh,
arrange blood stones under their beds
in patterns shamans would envy,
down extracts of marrow and cucumber,
potions promising a wonder fix,
the red cheeks and high fives
of good health. In extremis
the extreme appeals, offers the carnival ride
of another chance,
and until the immunological tumblers click
and champagne's popped in some lab,

there'll be a legion of gaunt believers
in the voodoo of the long shot,
their lives reduced
to the death-row philosophy
of nothing to lose.
Spes, the Roman goddess of hope,
holds a bud
that blooms to the light of her patient eyes.
Were we in the business of making gods today,
our Hope would be a hunter,
lean as fear
with bright and savage eyes.

Rivera's Golden Gate Mural

She's too young to care
why Chaplin's Great Dictator
balances the balloon-world,
or to grasp the political significance
of the mural's apportionment
into communities of soil and steel.
She likes the divers
arcing against the curve of time,
flattering them
by bending her back,
throwing out her arms,
cocking her head and looking down
as they do,
as if to say goodbye to the earth,
perhaps the first time she's sensed
flight's what the soul is after.
And in the prim girl
holding the wooden doll
she finds her *Doppelgänger,*
asking if I know her name
and if she's in the second grade
too, sensing
in her diminutive equal
her own shyness, a habit
of watching the world
while the world's not looking.
She doesn't ask about the American fist
clutching the wrist of fascism,
or notice Edison and Ford
touching the revolutions of their tinkering,
or perceive that, center of it all,

is a hybrid figure
of a stamping press and the goddess
Coatlicue,
an amalgam of appetites, human
and divine, a fusion-beast
that like the Sumerian lion-bird
touches something beyond
the schemata of reason,
an image from the realm
of nightmare or epiphany.
Finally she fixes on the tree
of Life and Love
rising from the joined hands of Rivera
and Paulette Goddard, Ziegfield girl
and movie star,
a tree that shines
like the glow-in-the-dark Duncan
I looped around the world
of my blackened childhood room.
She wants to know if trees
can really do this
and if this is what it was like
when her mother and I fell in love.
I don't tell her
what Frida Kahlo knew,
that it's never this simple,
or explain that she's the offspring
of a merely prosaic tenderness,
but say yes, without hedge
or qualification,
because I know a time will come
when the crap shoot of human relations
exhausts her,
and that if by then
she doesn't believe there's salvation

in the soft kiss at midnight,
or that a tree
in a dead man's painting
has something to tell her
about being alive,
art will be
but one more intimacy
she pushes aside.

Prodigal

You could drive out of this county
and attack the world with your ambition,
invent wonder plasmas,
become an artist of the provocative gesture,
the suggestive nod, you could leave
wanting the world and return
carrying it, a noisy bundle
of steam and libido, a ball of fire
balanced on your tongue,
you might reclaim Main Street in a limo
longer than a sermon, wave at our red faces
while remembering that you were born
a clod hopper, a farmer's kid,
and get over that hump once and for all
by telling A Great Man's stories —
the dirty jokes of dictators, tidbits
of presidential hygiene, insights
into the psychotropic qualities of power
and the American tradition of kissing
moneyed ass. Your uncle would still
call you Roy Boy, pheasants
sun themselves beside the tracks,
waiting for the dew to burn off
before their first flight, and corn
grow so high that if you stood
in the field you'd disappear, the fact
aiming your eyes down the road.

Surgery

Masked, they cut you, peel back
your skin for the legend of light
to enter your body. In this moment
they love you. You'll know this
years from now, when beating a rug
you feel their hands inside you,
a shock of warmth, invasion of concern,
as if you were back on the table
but awake and aware of the fear
dilating their eyes. How else can it be
for the strangers who take your breath,
contain it in a machine and give it back,
its meter undisturbed? They cut to flaw,
down to a blue tumor the size of an olive.
As they do they think of time, how little
it takes for the riotously dividing cells
to reach blood, to enter the cosmos
of a body and travel to another organ,
another world, advancing cancer's
parasitical flowering. Finally they try
to erase any sign they were there,
stitch and staple where they've cut.
If done well it's like walking backward
across a newly mopped floor. There
are only a few clues, in this case
a scar and the fact on any trivial day
                         you're still alive.

Duke

He was hit back of the head for a haul of $15,
a Diners' Club Card and picture of his daughter in a helmet
on a horse tethered to a pole that centered
its revolving universe. Pacing the halls, he'd ask

for a blow job he didn't want. The ward's new visitors
didn't know this request was all the injury
had left him to say, and would be shamed or pissed,
a few hitting him as he stood with his mouth

slightly open and large frame leaning in. His wife
divorced him for good and blameless reasons. He would not
be coming home to share his thoughts on film and weather,
or remember her any longer than it took to leave a room.

He liked ham. Kept newspapers in drawers and under his bed,
each unread page hand-pressed flat. And when it snowed
he leaned into one of the sealed, unbreakable windows,
a cheek to the cool glass as he held his fingers

over his mouth and moaned low and constant like the sound
of a boat on the far side of a lake. When he died
they cut him open to see how his habits had been rewired
and so tightly looped. Having known him they were afraid

of what can happen when you cross the lot to the office
or pull up to a light and thump the wheel as you might
any hour. If you stare at the dyed
and beautiful cross sections of a brain, it's natural

to wonder how we extract the taste of coffee
or sense of a note accurately found and held on an oboe
from this bramble. On Duke's slides they circled
the regions of blight which explain

why almost all behavior we recognize as human was lost,
but not why a man who'd curl into a ball
like a caterpillar when barely touched, could only ask
for sex, for intimacy, for the very thing

he could least accept and lived twelve years without,
no embrace or caress, no kiss on the lips before sleep,
until he died in the lounge looking out on a winter sky
that seemed eager to snow all day but didn't.

Memory

I hated the Road Runner.
I hated the Road Runner almost as much
as catching my father's knuckle ball.
And for whatever reason
these two displeasures became joined at the hip,
siamese tortures which still appear from time to time
on my psychic horizon.
TV's usually the trigger,
a chance encounter with the cartoon,
the theme song lodging in my cerebellum,
medulla oblongata
or whatever cranial nook it is
that absorbs the snatches of tunes
which loop us to insanity.
"Road Runner, the Coyote's after you.
Road Runner, if he catches you you're through."
Then I see the ball's
psychotic approach, the sphere jumping,
popping, weaving toward my shins or knees or thighs
or yes, higher still, so I can tell you
the joke about such an event creating a momentary soprano's
a lie, because each time I was too engrossed in moaning
to speak, let alone sing,
and would have been satisfied to live out my life
a monk, with a vocabulary of nods and gestures and safe
from the gonadal dangers of sport.
Memories often link umbilically.
Disraeli couldn't hear Big Ben without thinking of treacle.
I've a friend
who each time a jet flies by
remembers Miss Horton, his first grade teacher,

and her passion for the hokey pokey.
I thought of these things while reading about a man
imprisoned by mistake.
In the article he mentioned
the ten years of his wife's hard kisses he'd missed,
a son shot gunned in a drive-by
and the guards' refusal
to give him his suit and money back,
making him walk out of court in prison blues, broke
but staring into a free man's sunshine.
At home he took his blue three-piece,
blue jeans, even his blue socks
to the back yard, poured gas on the pile
and lit it with his brother's Zippo.
But it didn't work, he continued,
because any little thing
makes me remember, makes me feel
like I'm still in the joint, just another nigger
owned by time. The interviewer then asked
what he recalled most from his stay in prison.
That's easy, he said.
Everything.

Waiting

While waiting for the bus
I often review decisions I've made.
How at ten I refused to jump from a tree
when the others did, and so neither broke
my leg nor earned a blood-sealed handshake
from the older, sneering boys.
Or when I was requested by a woman
to wear a mask to bed
and deepen my voice into an ominous
snarl, and wouldn't, and was asked
to leave and not return until I'd inched
my libido into this century. Decisions
I do and do not regret, such as keeping
my nehru jackets, not committing
to disco as a philosophy of life,
oscillating in devotion
between the mystical reference points
of land and sea, settling finally
on an inclusive, undifferentiated awe.
And if the bus is late,
if it hasn't arrived by the time
I'm bored with my history,
I look dramatically forward and ask
what I'd do if the man next to me
were attacked or the sun began to fall
and I had time to extend a hand
in an attempt to deflect it
from a stranger; if I'd do
such a useless, essential thing as that.
I think I would, but remember
years ago watching a man beat his child

in a car outside a laundry,
that my response was to think
someone should do
something about that.

The Dead

They'll never kiss your forehead at midnight
as the moon chalks its zero
across the sky,
or kneel at the side of your bed
and whisper of the afterlife, their words
abundant as stars.

Still you rehearse, envision them next to you
on a porch,
the low sun dusting the earth gold,
or in a bar,
the table steepled with longnecks,
your fear liquored up
and the undertow of the juke box
pulling your reticent self
toward the accident
of honesty,
maybe they find you
late at night
at the kitchen table,
a bowl of peaches in the center,
placemats all around,
the dead
gabby as they never were
in life, unincumbered
by the impediment of flesh.

If you could embrace
or hover above the dead,
a lover licking their fingers
or judge
with a rat's black eyes,
you'd have your moments
of tenderness and retribution,
the chance to rub a friend's cancered chest,
to stand before the father
who beat you with the leg of a chair
and pain his eternity
with your unexpected forgiveness,
to smell your child's skin as it was in sunlight
or dance with your wife again
to the Dipper Mouth Blues,
to stare into the labyrinth of their eyes
until the visitation ends
and you're left alone with the moon,
which you've also taken for granted.

They'll never come,
though this won't keep you
from calling their names
when there's music in the elms
and you're snapped awake
by the dream that's trying to kill you.

Rearview Mirror

I saw her bounce on the passenger seat
at the red light as I dialed
from Aerosmith to Vivaldi to news,
a sequence interleaved with the aural dust
of static. She looked like a child
who could point four places at once,
whose first word was why, whose only
word was why, her body hyped
to interrogate the electric datum
of mailbox, blackbird, sky.
Her mother, the other player in this
silent film, rubbed both hands
over her face and drew them slowly
through her hair as we do
when we want the day's obstinate torments
to end. The little girl shook
her shoulder, and getting no response
shook it again. I looked away, up
at the light just then
turning green, and back in time
to see the woman's hand arc
from the wheel to the child's face,
the blow ovaling both their mouths
in surprise. Almost immediately
she folded her arms around the child
like mimosa closing on the day's
last packet of light. I drove off.
After one block they hadn't moved,
or two; after three I was reminded

by the traffic flowing about them
of those trees which split and grow
around the fence circumstance
has placed in their path.

Eight

We expect the perp to be stubbled or shined,
      Brook Brothers sharp or tattooed
with a fire-breathing beast we're to understand
          represents the terror of his soul,
that under the law's thumb he'll turn meek
      or smile as the camera zooms in
on the triumphal fuck-you of his life,

not that he sleeps with a Snoopy night-light on.
      But eight's ancient, some say,
it's down now to five, even four-year-olds
          rape, corner sisters, brothers and friends
and do what's been done to them, apples falling
      in the shadow of the tree. This kid
making news is said to have been molested

since jump, his parents' tag-team assault
      a shock to neighbors who describe them
as quiet and shy, though looking back,
          this revelation provided,
they deconstruct history, reinterpret the times
      their kids returned from his house
sullen or wild, dormant memories

that now explode in their imaginations,
      most looking as if they'd been awakened
by a hand around the throat. At the diner
          where I first read the story,
the regulars attack current events
      with cretinic certainty, share
between bites their Machiavellian intuitions

on the wielding of the foreign-aid carrot
       and military stick, argue
the pros and cons of the various perks
          one might choose to grease
local pols' palms, a clatch of pundits
       who've mapped the grassy knoll
and can reckon the effect of the President's sneeze

on the deutsch mark dollar tango, their shouts
       across the counter the dialectics
of those who hope by volume to achieve truth.
         Even they were stumped.
Confronted with images habit hasn't shaped the mind
       to associate with a child, they poked
hashbrowns and over-easys as the patterns

of familiar discourse failed, their usually
       decisive sentences tentative
and chopped, trailing off before the customary
        bravura, the declarations
of what's to be bombed and who's to be shot,
       one man offering this meek summation
to nods, that there's just something in him

that had to act this way. I took his "this way"
       with me, have kept it as one
keeps a stone in the pocket, to feel
        the contour and weight of the thing,
in this case the well-worn thought
       that there's bad we can't wash or think
or will away, sin woven into flesh,

evil laced between neurons, a notion
        I'm tested to apply to the rape
of a child by a child, finding nothing hermeneutic
           in the fact of flaw, the truism
that we're less than perfect, except comfort
        for those who believe we're made by birth
and not the days, who'd pull back

from the sloppy particular to the tidy
        indefinite, where the details
of any one life are cleanly lost and regret's
           the extent of what can sensibly
be offered. As I write, Montessori students
        teeter by my window, each roped by the hand
to the next, the entire train tethered to teacher,

a fiftyish woman whose eyes are hummingbirds
        flitting over the path, her being
devoted to perceiving the sly protocol of risk.
           This diminutive chain gang
passes every day, a chattering parable
        of innocence and need, most of the tots
oblivious to traffic and demonstrating

unmetered trust, reflexively turning toward
        any face because it's human, a faith
excluding few, the same naivete which allows them
           to be taken by the hand and walked
to basements and bedrooms. Soon these kids
        will sit at their desks, and sing,
count, and fill in the hollow people and things

of their coloring books, the farmer orange,
        the sun a chaos of red and green,
then listen, just before buses queue to take them home,
           as their teacher repeats the week's
strange lesson, the one about the good
        and the bad touch, when she'll breathe deep
and begin with the promise, Today we will learn.

85

I didn't expect this.
Windows, the ads for amazing
medical remedies, the recollection
of a stone washed flat by the river,
the one that skipped
eight times before its sleep . . .
I belong to these, and also limp,
cannot eat anything made with milk
or too much passion, hear little
of what is said (there are after all
always compensations), and still think
of what lies beneath a dress but without
the old results. I don't know
if it's a miracle or sin
that I can place my teeth
in a glass of water at night,
and wonder if this stranger's heart
sewn into my chest isn't lonely
and slowly dying of grief, if it
will simply stop and leave me
waving my arms in the air. I
didn't expect any of this,
the moments when I forget
a city, a person, and the days
made up of such moments, perhaps soon
the years, but I'm grateful
for the terror of these surprises,
given how it might have turned out,
given that I expect the alternative
to be nothing at all.

Alice Wakes at Two
and Looks Out the Window

A gate, she thinks,
I'm the gate
of my breathing,
of this powdery chant,
and I'll always mistake stars
for dust exploding
white in the noon sun.
They dance, those jewels,
as will I,
dance to the zoo
with my blue feet on,
with a silver drum,
dance bad words and hard tunes,
dance the colors men blush to.
Once there
I'll climb the fences,
seduce the alarms,
I'll move from lion
to monkey to lamb
and kiss the small packets
of their hearts.
Then come home to bed,
to warm eternity,
to the wheel
that twines my flesh
and spins it to sleep.
So fall, star,
and meet your embrace.
I'll name you True Love
and lick you with wishes.

530 Lakewood

When last in this house
the sun's blossoms covered my skin.
Now it spotlights a swastika
and the fisted zeroes of a punched out wall.
The new owners, capitalists of need and addiction,
leave their bottles, needles and condoms
wherever they want, heedless
of the adage concerning everything
and its place. Gone
is the banister my brother
split his chin on,
and the kitchen floor my mother
wrestled our shepherd across,
sympathizing with the rabbit
twisting between its teeth,
is torn up, burned, no longer
bears her proud, mirroring shine.
As some say, change changes change.
Yet here, on this doorjamb,
are the notches of my ascension,
a history of my inching
approach to the sun,
and there's the corner
where I'd curl and count
how often the Christmas lights flashed
before a door slammed
or the whoop or whine of a sibling
disturbed my favorite illusion,
that nothing existed in the world
but the fire of color
and the motor of my heart.

Now I'd like a voice to fill any corner
with proof my family had been here,
had devoted our souls
to the imperfect dramatization of love,
but silence
walks me out the door.
Leaving, I remember my mother
watching me leave, her following eyes
giving me an appetite for distance,
an inexplicable confidence in the word
beyond, and wish
the emissary of her ghost
would hover in a window, honoring,
subduing the myth of history,
the teetering event of this life.

Ten Years Dry

for L—

She misses the heft of rock and shot glass,
      vessels worthy of a sipped
gin & tonic or Seven and Seven slammed.
      Misses the chromatic smorgasbord
of a vigorous backbar. Misses that little
      step up and onto the stool,
strength of mahogany under her hands, the gap
      between setting smokes
and lighter down and the first taste,
      that moment of expectation
when the head-grind stopped and she heard
      the bar's braided voices
as chorus, her breathing slowed by the company
      of laughter carved into the air.
This fondness for artifact and moment comes
      after ten years red-knuckling
the blood-shot hours, reminiscence a prize
      like steady hands, job, friends,
trophy of the patched soul that woke too often
      scratching for the name
of the bottom feeder snoring beside her. Bar
      was home. Terminus. Mecca.
The jukebox read her mind, matched her cycles
      of melancholy and rage.
Bartenders mumbled like shot transmissions
      or genuflected before trauma
and wound. Failure was expected, rewarded,
      tolerance shown for the saga
of snag, the lost job, black eye; even
      the hauntings of second selves,
of raped and ass-kicked ghosts, were looked upon
      as standard issue, what anyone

picks up along the way. She even misses
       the knife-edged tenderness
of drunks, the crapulous stumble, heave,
       psychotic jubilee of DTs,
the gut-clutched roll when every drop roared down
       as poison. Because they evolved
to a last drink, when with sunlight sprawled
       on the bar, she caught her face
in the mirror and set the full and beautiful
       glass down. Victorious. Having
finally killed who she'd been after all along.

AIDS

I tried visiting home.
They're such delicate people,
butterflies really,
quiet in a way
that reminds me of rain,
of the soft breath of sleep.
When Dad shook my hand
there was a tension to his skin
like exists inside every wind,
a desire to move forward and back
at the same time,
to touch and eradicate.
And when my mother kissed me
I cried in the way we sometimes do —
no tears, a burning force
behind the face,
pain turned upon itself,
a kind of emotional cannibalism —
because I felt
the slight trembling of her lips,
a stoic's most powerful expression
of fear and impotence.
We ate,
walked around the edge of the field,
talked about the season,
the neighbors,
the moon.
My mother swore
that through the years
it's become bigger,
and she laughed and said
          But maybe it's just my eyes.

I wanted to assure them
I'd been loved,
that there'd been someone
whose hand I'd held,
whose weaknesses I'd never betrayed.
How is it that people exist
so far apart,
that we stand a hand away
yet look upon each other
as ghosts,
as dust we love
yet cannot see or reach.
We looked at the stars come out,
in bunches, in leaps and swirls,
and I could say nothing,
could move no nearer,
no farther away.
I left the next morning,
afraid if I stayed
they'd cry,
cry and shatter
to look at me,
because I know they feel
it's somehow their fault,
that even this
they should have been able
to protect me from.
If only I could convince them,
could say something
which might work its way
into their sleep,
their hearts,
and soothe, and solace.
But all I can think of
is that you love as you have to
and die the best you can.

My Job as It Relates to Bruegel's
Netherlandish Proverbs

I am today
        figure 105 as labeled
in *The Art of Mixing Metaphors.*
I've also been pillar biter and hen toucher,
have dragged the block and run
through the wheat with my pants on fire,
a misplaced swine-flock scattering before me,
have shat on the gallows
and had a toothache behind the ears,
though not for the thinnest slice of time
spun the world on my thumb, well-sucked
as it is. In the painting I lean my head
against a red brick wall, left foot bare
and right hand clutching a knife, suggesting
that except for my obvious imbecility
I mean business, am ready to kick life's ass
the moment I overcome
my quibbling quantum difficulties
and push through this wall. The madness
of this sport's the very lesson
bureaucrats have taught me today
with their phone-maze of churlish greetings
and endlessly branching
push-button options,
the telecommunical equivalent
                of quicksand, is
the philosophical fool's gold I'm left
after trying to diminish the list
of things-to-be-done, only to find
it feeds on my efforts and grows

with embryonic intensity, a life-form
evolving the attributes of consciousness
and spite. I could learn much
from the man who carries the day out
in a bucket. As he steps from his door,
another load of sunlight steaming
in his pail, he looks
                              happy, pleased by the pace
of his busy work, much as the woman
tying the devil to a pillow has a glow
of satisfaction, beams with the sense
of a job well done. And of course
I look up to the man who shoots arrows
through the roof. It's hard work
threading the shafts one after another
through the same tiny hole,
yet he rarely stops. When he does
it's to drag an arm across his face
and look toward the sea
as if he owns this country.
Even from here I'm stunned
by the militancy of this
                              shy boast.

Voladores

Literally, voladores means "fliers,"
but the literal is the least of the matter.
— *Gene S. Stuart*

They fly, bodies suddenly light,
bones hollow as birds'. Four
voladores are waist-tied to ropes
wound around the top of a pole

and fed through a revolving frame.
As they fall back and spin away
they become the winds that bite
God's tongue, that stroke

the bronze clay. Having fasted.
Having dreamed without sleeping.
A fifth dances on top of the pole.
Think of this person as the center

of the universe. The hush at the core
of matter's outward scream. Gravity's
the engine of this machine, balance
the flywheel. But we believe in hands

as wings, that the feathers sewn
to their shirts are their souls
flowering through skin. Long ago
this rite was performed beside

a human sacrifice. Killed with arrows
as the voladores circled down,
the victim's blood was offered
to Tlazolteotl, mother of all gods,

then scattered as rain for crops.
Reaching the ground the fliers
would run around the pole, their wings
dripping color, while above them

the universe still danced. Today
a turkey's killed instead of a man,
its blood pooling black in the dirt.
Flies have at it. Modest, modern gods

are wooed by this small appeasement:
entering the voladores, the husks
of their skulls, they replace
their human thoughts with a hawk's,

their blunt eyes with a crow's
black pearls. Whirling around the pole,
we hear their bodies whickering air.
By the time they reach ground

they'll be dead as men, though in word
and flesh they'll seem the same.
It is their shadows that will walk
amid ours as predators among prey.

Traffic Jam

I try to make eye contact with a pig.
I see rumps and flanks, snouts
through the flesh-hauler's metal mesh,
but no eyes and therefore no piggy soul
greets me. We who were speeding
now inch toward fate, fabled endpoint
when spoils will be allotted and heads
chopped off. We think of change as waiting
ahead, a leash dragging us forward. Onward
occidental soldiers. The next installment
may well be mundane, tar slingers patching
the long slink of highway, or deadly,
iron jaws chewing at a Nova's collapsed door
as a man struggles to remember the one prayer
he knows. Condensed, it goes something like
Our Father, save my ass. The pigs
will soon fulfill their bacon and pork rind
destiny. Their stench is a hook through my nose.
Probably the farmer doesn't mind. He smells
cash, knows his shoes and snow tires
are gifts of swine. In some psychic stratum
his identity and theirs have fused,
fostering a love similar to a painter's
infatuation with her fat tubes of color.
On the highway the jostling begins. From the air
it'd look like a loom, cars strung out
like multi-colored threads. And here he comes,
the inevitable throttle-jock in a Vette
or Trans Am who figures going eighty's
even easier when everyone else sits still.
He'll cut through us like a ginsu knife,

like a neutrino on its way to forever being
on its way. Arrival is the issue. When will we get
where, and will what's happening there
play like the cinema of our dreams? I'm learning
to accept these moments as lesson. Slow down.
Take time to smell the pigs. Try to look one
in the eye, feel the press of its stubborn being
against mine. Let what's behind me catch up.
The woman bearing nature's smile. The kid
endlessly waving because he's just learned
an open palm cracks the shell of others' lives.
The man crying because the radio's sent him
a song from adolescence, a true love tune
he thought he'd outgrown but sings with a teenager's
sob-packed fury. As traffic stops some get out
to inspect stasis. With horn blasts come pig squeals.
Somewhere John Cage taps a dead man's foot, pleased
by the music of happenstance. I close my eyes
and accept the idle of the pig truck as the blather
of a river. What we say to rivers they say back.
This makes us feel less alone, not so afraid.
I picture the person who'll shoot or stun the pigs
singing to them, even stroking them once, quickly
though delicately, an assembly line of slaughter
and devotion. It's my way of imagining a hand
filling mine with confidence at the end.

Random Events

Tom Emery, according to the paper,
was arrested with a match
in his hand. Because of the nature
of Mr. Emery's crime, he'll be tested
to determine if voices compel him
to seek attention in theatrical ways,
if he feels an eye floating above
and following him, an eye like
the giant spider's in Johnny Quest,
if he masturbates too frequently
or not enough, if he can make
sanctioned sense of ink stains
and believes what the sane
and Catholic do about God, that
the Creator knows and controls
everything, loves each soul and stick
on this blessed planet, and still
lets us go mad and put children
in ovens. Theodicy, it's called,
a verification of the goodness of God
despite the existence of evil
in the world. My guess is Mr. E.
doesn't, that his test results
will stretch the psychiatric bell curve
and prove him a resident of the statistical
fringe, at home in the psychic territory
of poodle torturers and necrophiles.
But this is a story of luck,
for at the feet of Tom Emery the cops
found a pile of defective blue-tips,
eight matches that wouldn't pop

into flame. Usually we hear
when it works the other way.
The bolt snaps in the jet engine,
the tracks give out, the bridge
buckles, events overcome the studies,
schematics, the analyses of stress and shear,
a confluence of circumstances
changing the odds from never
to now. The boy will perhaps be haunted
by a nebulous dread, a need
to hurt whatever's warm and trusting,
or will play catch behind the house of loving,
adoptive parents, and come to believe
gentleness alone thrives. Probably
he'll never be told, though if he is
it'll only be a matter of time
before he asks if the match was lit
when the cops kicked down the door
and came screaming inside.

Visiting The Wall

Yet leaving here a name, I trust,
That will not perish in the dust.
—*Robert Southey*

The sweet gum
hover in the granite,
an onyx mirror in which our faces
also float with the names.
One end pointing
to Washington's obelisk, the other

to Lincoln's temple,
the monument forms a gentle V,
arms sloping downward,
a descent
as would have been made by visitors
to Agamemnon's tomb. People flow

in both directions,
two streams of Nikons, roses
and back-packs, babies crying
or awed by light,
men in fatigues whose tears
and hard-set lips, the animate sorrow

of warriors,
offer counterpoint to the wall's
arrested recognition. I grew up
a voyeur of this war,
the invoice of body count,
theatre of massacre and immolation,

delivered each night
as I bent over a TV tray, the wounds
surprising, not clean
          like Gunsmoke's
or the Rat Patrol's
but revolutionary in their sloppy realism.

A man wearing a beret
wheels up, leans near and fingers a name.
I remember being eight
          and coming in
from catching fireflies,
the shocking switch from suburban twilight

to a helicopter
whirring above the exotic menace I knew
as Vietnam, a man twitching
          while another pushed
against his stomach,
trying to keep what was inside

in, and realize
this marine and his fellows were also
voyeurs, witnesses of sights
          no one should see,
the imaginative cruelty
of a bomb trip-wired to a baby,

the sport
of genital collection, a dozen men
skinned and hung from a tree.
          The poem he leaves joins
other gifts, the turquoise teddy
with white lace trim, pack of Beemans,

whoopee cushion,
the polaroid of a boy whose small afro's
a halo catching sun,
the stratocaster with an amp cord
plugged in, American flag
taped to the other end, the stars blacked out

with a felt-tip pen,
the See 'n Say with pictures
of John Foster Dulles, Johnson,
Nixon and Thieu
glued over the animals,
the Royal typewriter, a model

salesmen stood on
to demonstrate its toughness,
Sharon Lane typed once on a sheet
of onion skin before each key
was snapped off, the watch
hammered at 12 : 31, offerings reflecting

the common genius
for loss, how well love recalls
the details contouring personality,
the delimiting particulars
of the adored. Finally it's the names
I notice, how in aggregate they numb

but individually
touch, sparking a desire to read the role,
to speak Conrad Lee Flyinghorse,
James Thomas Moses,
George J. Economus, if only
to the air, an act impulsed

by the beauty
of all names, the sound of Max
            Edward Nimphie Jr., Daniel Savage,
                David Floyd Able,
            Paul Ross Savacool Jr.,
each an utterance predating

            this war,
their first smokes and blushing kisses,
                when it was decided
                        how the world would know
                a child so hopefully,
so violently born.

Ohmy

I do my part for ignorance
by believing certain things.
That the sun rises.
That children
come innocent and slowly
grow to corruption.
That perseverance
will outshine talent.
That I must die.
Once it was held
that a man in the moon
seduced women
and they bled.
That the sun
was a ball of fire
the size of a Greek island.
That if a corpse
were passed through a window
and carried around the house
three times,
the soul of the deceased
would forget how to enter
and leave the inhabitants in peace
with their meat, vegetables
and suspicion.
The point of this
seems to be
to believe nothing,
to make no pact with facts,
numbers, and especially
those tales we tell

of origins and outcomes,
the theories
we so willingly take to bed.
This is wisdom.
This is impossible.

Divorce

The complaints of the man on the phone
transport me to restaurants,
foreign countries, tiny inns
on postcard lakes. He speaks
with the intimacy common
on talk shows, revealing secrets
that should only be shared
with millions of thoughtful,
clinically trained strangers.
So I begin to think of guns, unusual
because I've never fired or held
or even viewed any part of my anatomy
as one, begin to feel that, though
we're friends, I'll hang up,
get in my car and speed across the nation,
knock softly on his door
and when he answers,
let my reptilian brain take over
and devise a strategy of pain
that'll humble him into remembering
that once and for a very long time,
he loved the woman he's now degrading,
and that together they chose to make
something more of that love
than a Club Med weekend. After the call,
I get into bed and spoon behind my wife,
hoping that if either of us
tires of the other and hires an attorney,
begins sorting through books and albums,
finds a little place with a wood stove
and a view of the highway, we don't spew

revisionist history, suggest the other
whinnied in their sleep or found latex
irresistible, but have the grace
to be honestly miserable, to break the bond
without trashing the beloved.
When she asks what's wrong, I begin to say
idiots, we're all idiots, but stop
and put my arms around her. Because
we're not, and because warmth's
better comfort than words.

Learning of "It"

It was disgusting. In the basement
my brother casually described the space
in my mother my father had filled
to make me, drew a poor likeness
of a vagina on cardboard, the pencil point
quivering over the corrugated veneer
as labial lines and a pubic thatch
took shape, my brother breaking
amid his anatomical doodling to predict
that I'd come to crave this as much
as I did peanut butter and jelly,
which is to say, more than life itself.
A doltish nine, this bit of sex-ed
shocked, my reply a series
of authoritative denials, as in
no way man, not me, not
ever, a little fit I rolled up the ramp
of pre-hormonal pique and shouldered
off the end, concluding
with an oath that summoned devastation
upon my sacred gadgets and dreams
if I ever so much as thought
of doing as he described, a promise
it's been my good fortune not to keep.
My conversion was mundane, an instance
of the same strange attractor
working through the example of my flesh
as has tweaked countless lovers,
a psycho-sexual ah-ha brought on
when I realized something had happened
to certain seventh grade girls,

the abrupt rounding
of their plane figures over summer
persuading me as my brother's art work
never could that how I got here
depended on the fact
that a calf or breast could seem
an infinite space and eyes
look back without hurry, my first inkling
sight functions as embrace. By the time
I made love I'd seen my share
of glossy spreads and heard
the blustery testimonials to pussy, prize one
amid the array of sham tokens
brokering boys to men. I never got
this totemic need to note and notch
or would want such tattling
turned on me, but will divulge
that when I was finally and tenderly
proved wrong, the most vital surprise
came after, as we talked and she made
not the slightest move
to clothe or cover, an openness
effecting ease, allowing anything to be said,
when we lolled for hours
in the fat afternoon light, through dusk,
until night, when I could no longer tell
where her body ended or words began.

Nigger

It was a new word and as words went then
astonishing. After popping
in the air it fell like the silence of a sheet

snapped out over a bed. Reaching
the flanneled back
of a man leaving the store, it paralyzed him,

gripped his stride and the swing of his arms
in the cast
of a momentary statue. From the thicket

of belts I could see half-moon smiles
rise over the Sunday
stubbled chins of men huddled at the counter.

When the man had gone they laughed except
for my father
and one other, who set pliers, picture hooks

and nine volts on the counter and walked away.
Each head turned
to follow him as if blown by the same wind.

As he passed in front of the tube-tester,
someone shouted
exotic words which tore the air like a bike

skidding on gravel. The door opened magically
as he approached
and was closed some time before the owner

slammed the register drawer, releasing them
from the space
they'd been staring at, a bit of air bounded

by rakes and lawnmowers through which
they'd each soon pass
after paying what was asked for what was wanted.

Nurse

She thinks of him as a pancake.
        He says nothing as she turns him over,
has said nothing in two years.
                He reminds her of soaps
in which someone's often dying,
                someone important or ecstatically loved,
                        usually a well-tanned man
whose been wounded doing something

terribly, excitingly wrong.
        Typically they're attended by a nurse
who's never seen blood, who's there
                to suggest the constancy
of erotic potential. Such scenes
                she compares to her life, his life,
                        the man she washes
each day and thinks of as a god

smooth as breath.
        Confessing to his arms, hands,
to the black pebbles lodged in his eyes,
                she admits that at times
she dreams her house burns while her husband
                and daughter sleep inside,
                        that she does nothing
but wave, wave as if they're leaving

on a cruise, and gets up
        the next day, still loving them,
still confused. She thinks of him as an ally,
        as a pet. Each day while she rubs
his bony hands, the long trail
        of each arm, the papyrus
                of his cheeks, she imagines
he's about to speak. Once

she even kissed the scar on his neck,
        felt his pulse against her lips,
cadence of his obstinate flesh,
        and knew then he'd always remain
the quiet preceding thunder,
        the silence which flows
                before the many voices
of the fleeting rain.

Man of the House

It was a misunderstanding.
I got into bed, made love
with the woman I found there,
called her honey, mowed the lawn,
had three children, painted
the house twice, fixed the furnace,
overcame an addiction to blue pills,
read Spinoza every night
without once meeting his God,
buried one child, ate my share
of Jell-o and meatloaf,
went away for nine hours a day
and came home hoarding my silence,
built a ferris wheel in my mind,
bolt by bolt, then broke it
just as it spun me to the top.
Turns out I live next door.

The Shrine

Twice a week I baby-sat six
schizophrenics, fed them macaroni
   and meds, wrote novellas
for the state, narratives
of their cognitive fits and lock-ups,
   and like a gentleman

lit their gaspers, mainly menthols,
nicotine a staple, smoke a language
   climbing the air.
S — was a rambler whose jabber
was punctuated, exclamated
   by the clairvoyant's zing,

who'd break her rap on the eyes
which hounded her, on the TV
   which hummed and snapped
like an accusation, to say what I'd felt
since waking, since childhood,
   since turning from the window,

from the grey light of Michigan's
sedative sky. As I entered her room
   one night, she pulled her bed
from the wall to reveal a small shrine,
the body of Christ made of foil and hair
   of bread-bag twisters,

a toothpaste sky on cardboard
backdropping Calvary,
          the skull-shaped hill
made of coffee grounds, moldy by then,
His flat hands pin-pierced, a doll's
          bloodless stigmata,

and rocks, bottle caps, paper clips
and soap pressed and glued
          into a ringing wall.
After a jag of bible-speak
she took my hand and held it
          to her cheek, cool

as a river wind, and calmly said,
They all join Him, as if she knew
          of my sister recently dead
from diabetes, a knowledge conveyed
by scent or resonance, the mute witness
          of flesh. That

she instantly hopped to another subject,
faded into the wash of her own noise,
          gave the moment
a puritan intimacy, as if she'd said
all that needed to be said
          and had now to get on

with the cruel work of madness.
Such kindness I returned with pop
          and cookies, walks
around the grounds, my hand
when she sat piled in a corner,
          eyes wide, head

swinging side to side, deflecting
the images that attacked her
      or trying to avoid,
to slip away from the sound of air
cracking, the quivering thread of light
      stripped to core.

And sometimes I'd sit beside her, eyes
closed, and listen to the baroque
      runnel of her words
until she was silent, when often
I found myself nodding as if to music
      or a simple truth.

Ice Storm

Ice cakes, shears by weight,
        deforms the deciduous guard
lining the street. With each
        slow loss tension builds

nearly sexually, a progression
        audible, divisible
into creak, moan, crack,
        the end crisp as a fast ball

off a big league bat. Despite
        concern we're giddy.
It's a good show, violent
        and lovely at once,

combining the lottery's
        random zing
with the drama of localized
        disaster, just the thing

to snap winter's chain
        of xeroxed days.
Power loss turns us kids,
        candle-tranced and tingling

with illicit thrill,
        who snub sleep, the requisite
eight, to sill-prop elbows
        and browse the dazzling array,

matter's plurality
        crystal-sheathed, democracy
in action, the ambient light
        magnified, acclaimed by ice,

waves of shivering quanta
        clobbering our eyes. Have trees
mind, a shred of cellular
        consciousness, can they receive

this maiming's beauty
        as recompense, flagellants
with hands upturned to God?
        I can't help but see

the litter of limbs as human.
        They cue an image
of left arms hacked and piled
        by Cambodian parents

after their tots' Red Cross
        inoculations, shots feared
as pestilence, carriers
        of Western voodoo. There's

no secluded fact. Presented one
        we seek kin, literal,
metaphorical, categorical, a stew
        to mix our thoughts in.

A healthy maple splits, screams
        as it goes, rage
orchestrating its fall,
        the glittering cascade.

What stands is gimped, leans
           in apparent bereavement,
won't live to shade summer's walk.
           Tomorrow, devastation's sheen

melted, we'll play pick-up sticks,
           bend through breath's fog
for branch and twig, pile the remains
           curbside, mass one proof

the world's changed. The other's
           mind-sketch, spine-trace,
memories remodeled by the stories
           we'll tell, each unique

as snowflake, our takes
           on where we were, what
we felt, how it sounded the night
           even the luminous air fell.

Front Porch, Listening

No longer reading of Liège,
corpses yard high on the glacis,
German bayonets
        countering Belgian bullets
with expected result,
I eavesdrop as my neighbor
suggests to her husband
        they summer at Gull Lake.
Other books on my lap,
I've heard her ask this man,
ten years dead, the sensible
        and surreal,
if he remembered
the chorus to Carolina Moon
or knows why night
        hangs smooth as it does.
That I can't hear him's
not her fault,
just as Joan of Arc,
        confessing at Rouen
to the visitations
of Saints Catherine,
Michael, and Margaret
        couldn't have overcome
her inquisitors deafness,
that clerical incapacity
to grasp the tones
        of passionate belief.
Lithium might mute his voice,
and she'd be thought
better off, her mind
        realigned with the truth,

which is that the dead
don't sit with us
and recommend zinnias
            when we mention
the garden's imbalance,
its inability to infatuate.
And it is mad wisdom
            to chat with air,
yet consider how promptly
our bickering and guffaws,
the puns and pet names
            which transform breath
into humanity,
dissipate into a silence
that doesn't hint
            we were here.
In my book
the Great War's begun.
Millions die in a paragraph.
            And while their voices
escape me, my right mind
hears in the wind
the tone poem
            of their last words.

Forecast

I fell asleep in the rain.
Its too many kisses
washed my face away.
I thought it a dream,
but woke with little
to offer mirrors.
Now the sky
is clear.
However
the forecast
is for rain.
These are shoes,
this is my shirt,
this a list
of my sins,
my little pleasures.
Remember them.
Soon they'll be
what's left of me.

A Night at Modern Prototype

Waleid drew a map of Lebanon, x'ed where his village
used to be. Paradise, he said, his English
sustaining no more sacred word, then dropped the lunch bag
into molten steel, its flame sudden as a meteor
burning through atmosphere, earth's invisible skin.
This was also the night the foreman showed me
a Playboy fold-out and asked, "Well?", confiding
he intended to meet and marry the woman who smiled
with erotic fury through the pain of her stapled thigh.
After the usual comments, he shyly risked explaining
her eyes, the kind of kindness he found there, a quality
he'd still be unable to finger the night he heard
she was shotgunned, though he'd drink enough to try.
That shift I stoned a punch for a Mustang door,
straddled the casting and ground its surface
smooth, rocked into a trance which ate the hours
and pushed away, as rocking does for any child,
all the things I might have cried for. We knocked off
early, at 3 AM shared a tall-boy and cigarettes
under a straight-up moon, our fatigued bodies
trying to float away, the talk of politics, chest pains,
Carl's junkie son, who wanted both to be beaten
and embraced, saved from and slipped into
his father's shoes. In two hours the day shift
would pick up the ladles and chains we'd held that night
and do exactly as we had, burn and mill steel
into the shapes of things that'd make other things,
each of us gods of a tiny world, the few actions
we'd repeat long enough to call it a life.

With five minutes till punch out we'd talked our way
down to silence. I could hear trucks whine on the highway
and crickets in the field, their rhythm steady as a machine,
constant as a heart that does no more than it's asked to.

Dogfish Mother

a Haidan deity

Dogfish Mother has a hawk's nose and teeth
for two. When she talks
I feel her words in my stomach, a thrashing
like crows live there.
She sits with her eyes closed until night,
when it's time
to repair the sky with naming. When I last
visited Dogfish Mother,
we sat on the roof and she pointed out a few
of the white constellations.
She did this to shame them. Then she showed me
man-laughing-with-pants-down,
woman-pounding-clothes-on-a-rock, wolf-eating-baby,
cat-swallowing-face.
Such an appetite she admires. She says gods
aren't archers or charioteers.
Gods have lice, drink whiskey, leave the mule
two weeks tied up
and unfed, and sometimes fall asleep in a chair,
each dream the shell
of a blue world. Dogfish Mother has a shark's eyes,
black as a burnt wick
and quick to seize flaw, to see that a limp's
from a fight or smile
a trap door. Because she can fly she's a moon
tattooed on my shoulder.
If I drink too much I tell her, if I need
to touch a woman
I tell her, when each thought's a gun
held to my temple
I tell her because she already knows. Truth

rounds her eyes,
her gaze spreads over me like a river.
Lie and she squints,
stares until a blade slides across my throat.

Your Daughter

When she phones at two
        stammering the boyfriend's name
and the list of ingested riches, a potion
                of three-dollar wine, blotter
and pills she calls Bullets
                but you remember as Black Beauties,
once your own by-the-handful favorite, after

she counts the range
        you ask her to, gives her address
and describes her bedroom's layout,
                convincing you an ambulance
is unnecessary drama,
                when you work out directions
to a town some two hours away and down

a dirt road
        to a party store with a Dr. Pepper sign
advertising an iced benediction against its side,
                you deliver your wife
the Cliff Notes version
                of the worn tale, tell her
it's your turn and wish her back to a sleep

she won't find.
        Driving, you recall your own
haze-days, how you stunned yourself into seeming
                epiphanic bliss, moments
of zealous and random intention,
                ratcheted your mind
to what felt its quivering core, the reason

never grasped,
   your parents kind and moderately hip,
school a snap, your psyche, according to the pros'
    probes, only conventionally
glitched. It was just something you did, something
    she's doing now, a path
she swears you can't understand

because she was born
   after the tracks had healed and you'd last
licked coke from a mirror. Best
    you can, you try and space the groundings
sensibly, to scream strategically, when you see
    something open in her eyes,
that cloud roll back you once

lived under,
   to say nothing most of the time
because that's what you remember hearing. Pulling up,
    she's slumped against the phone booth,
her gaze a rodeo, speech a voracious dissertation
    stumbling on the pedestrian thicket
of language. You sit next to her

and listen
   as the prehistoric light of stars
touches your skin with immeasurable indifference,
    put your arms around her as she rocks
against the solid history of your flesh,
    though tomorrow on the stairs
you'll make room to avoid the slightest touch.